KEIKO ABE

安倍圭子　マリンバ・ダモーレ

Marimba d'amore

for marimba solo

SCHOTT

SJ-051

記譜法：

♩ (× notehead) ＝マレットのヘッドを打ったまま音板に押しつけ、響きを消す。

♩ (✱ notehead) ＝音板の端をマレットの柄の部分で打つ。

♩ (✱ notehead with bounce) ＝音板の端をマレットの柄の部分で打った後にそのまま自然にバウンドさせる。
（音が複数になる）

この作品は、5オクターヴの音域のマリンバのために書かれているが、5オクターヴの音域を持たない楽器で演奏する場合は、4, 12, 15ページを巻末の楽譜を使って演奏することができる。

演奏時間：10分

NOTATION：

♩ (× notehead) ＝Strike bar and keep mallet head pressed against it.

♩ (✱ notehead) ＝Strike edge of bar with handle of mallet.

♩ (✱ notehead with bounce) ＝Strike edge of bar with handle of mallet and then let handle bounce naturally.

This work was written for a marimba with five octaves. When using an instrument that does not have a compass of five octaves, pages 4, 12, and 15 can be performed using the score at the end of the book.

Duration: 10 minutes

Marimba d'amore

マリンバ・ダモーレ

for marimba solo

Keiko Abe
安倍圭子

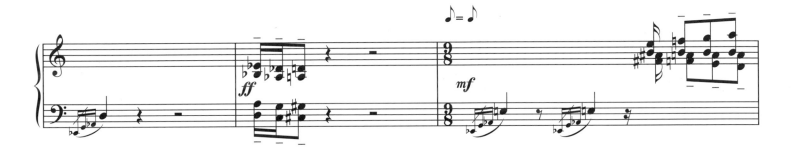

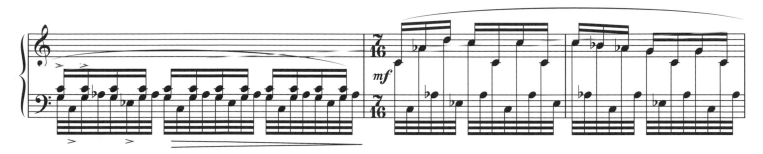

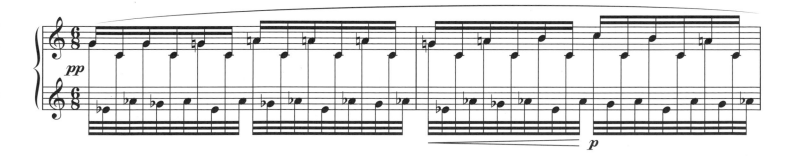

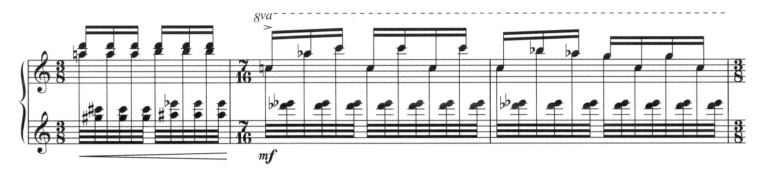

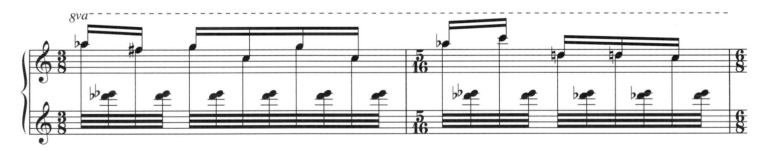

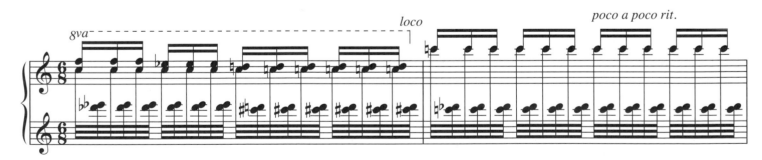

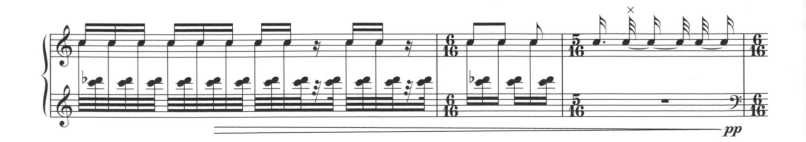

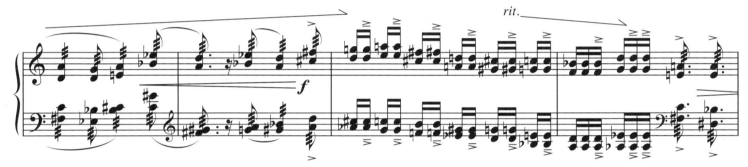

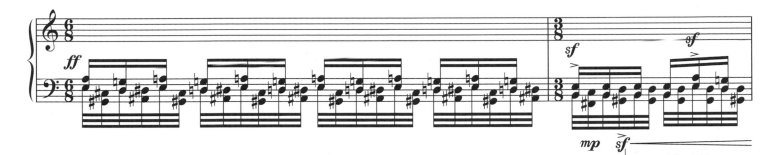

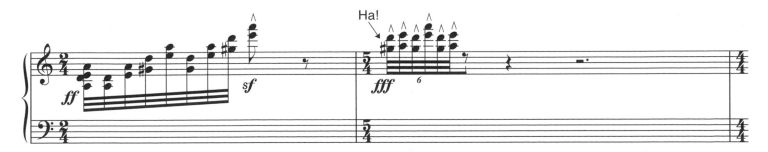

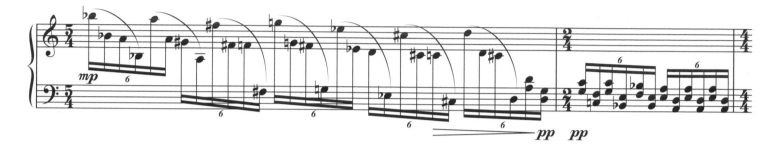

poco accel.

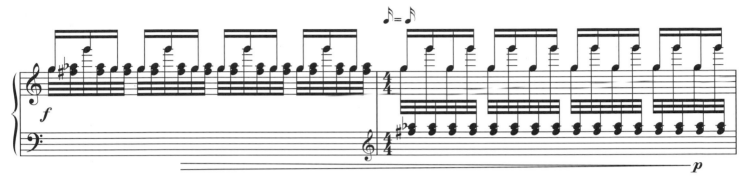

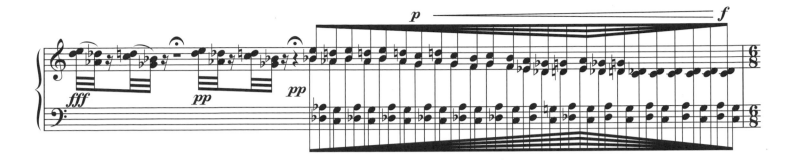

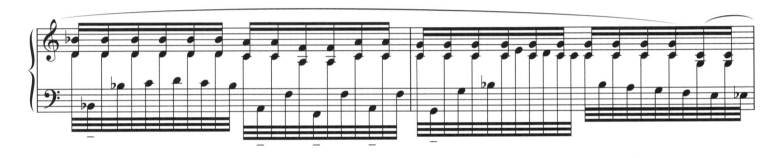

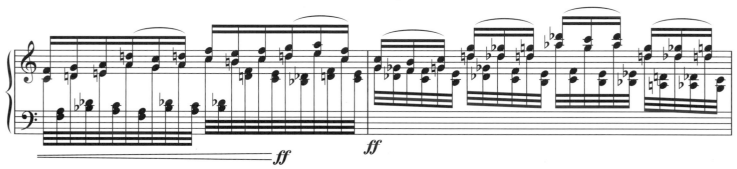

Più mosso
Con energia

allargando

U!

音域の狭いマリンバのために

この作品は、5 オクターヴの音域のマリンバのために書かれているが、5 オクターヴの音域を持たない楽器で演奏する場合は、4, 12, 15 ページを以下の楽譜を使って演奏することができる。

For marimba with narrow compass

This work was written for a marimba with five octaves. When using an instrument that does not have a compass of five octaves, pages 4, 12, and 15 can be performed using the following score.

Marimba d'amore
マリンバ・ダモーレ
for marimba solo

Keiko Abe
安倍圭子

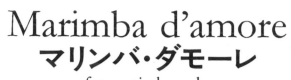

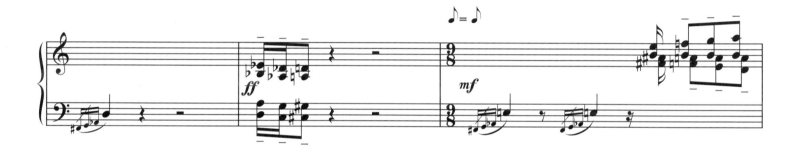

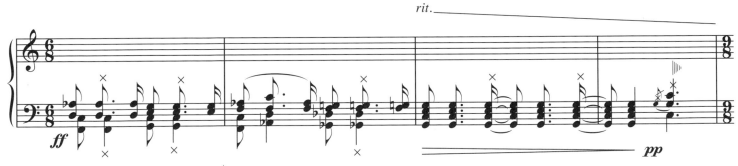

（編集上、空白にしています。）

(For editorial reasons, left blank.)

Più mosso
Con energia

（編集上、空白にしています。）

(For editorial reasons, left blank.)

安倍圭子《マリンバ・ダモーレ》　　　　　　　　　●

初版発行————————————————————2001年6月25日
第3版第1刷⑤————————————————2016年5月31日
発行—————————————————————ショット・ミュージック株式会社
　—————————————————————東京都千代田区内神田1-10-1 平富ビル3階
　—————————————————————〒101-0047
　—————————————————————(03)6695-2450
　—————————————————————http://www.schottjapan.com
　—————————————————————ISBN 978-4-89066-051-3
　—————————————————————ISMN M-65001-177-8

現代の音楽
MUSIC OF OUR TIME

安倍圭子　KEIKO ABE

マリンバ作品集
遙かな海／竹林／小さな窓／古代の壺／わらべ歌による譚章
Works for Marimba
Memories of the Seashore／Wind in the Bamboo Grove／Little Windows／Ancient Vase／Variations on Japanese Children's Songs
for marimba . . . SJ 050 . . . 2400円

マリンバ・ダモーレ
Marimba d'amore
for marimba . . . SJ 051 . . . 1600円

マリンバ二重奏曲集
遙かな海Ⅱ／竹林Ⅱ
Works for Marimba Duo
Memories of the Seashore Ⅱ／Wind in the Bamboo Grove Ⅱ
for marimba duo . . . SJ 052 (performing score) . . . 1400円

武満 徹　TORU TAKEMITSU

雨の樹
Rain Tree
for 3 percussion players . . . SJ 1006 (score & parts) . . . 4500円

クロス・ハッチ
Closs Hatch
for marimba and vibraphone . . . SJ 1144 (performing score) . . . 700円

細川俊夫　TOSHIO HOSOKAWA

想起
Reminiscence
for marimba . . . SJ 1160 . . . 1200円

湯浅譲二　JOJI YUASA

相即相入第二番
Interpenetration No.2
for two percussionists . . . SJ 1021 (performing score) . . . 2000円

冬の日・芭蕉讃
A Winter Day ―Homage to Bashô―
for flute, clarinet in B♭, percussion, harp and piano . . . SJ 1028 (performing score) . . . 1400円

一柳 慧　TOSHI ICHIYANAGI

源流
The Source
for marimba . . . SJ 1061 . . . 1600円

《バラード》と《グリーン・リズム》
Ballade and Green Rythms
for marimba . . . SJ 1168 . . . 1900円

森の肖像
Portrait of Forest
for marimba . . . SJ 1018 . . . 1200円

パガニーニ・パーソナル
Paganini Personal
for marimba and piano . . . SJ 1013 (performing score) . . . 2000円

リズム・グラデーション
Rhythm Gradation
for timpani . . . SJ 1104 . . . 2200円

展望Ⅱ
Perspectives Ⅱ
for percussion . . . SJ 1097 . . . 1300円

風の軌跡
Wind Trace
for 3 keyboard percussion . . . SJ 1031 (performing score) . . . 2000円

トリオ・インターリンク
Trio Interlink
for violin, piano and percussion . . . SJ 1068 (performing score) . . . 2600円

リカレンス
Recurrence
for flute, clarinet, percussion, harp, piano, violin and cello . . . SJ 1020 (performing score) . . . 2800円

権代敦彦　ATSUHIKO GONDAI

木はやはりなにも言わない
wood still says nothing
for marimba . . . SJ 1155 . . . 1500円

ショット・ミュージック株式会社
東京都千代田区内神田1-10-1　平富ビル3階　〒101-0047
電話 (03) 6695-2450　ファクス (03) 6695-2579
sales@schottjapan.com　http://www.schottjapan.com

SCHOTT MUSIC CO. LTD.
Hiratomi Bldg., 1-10-1 Uchikanda, Chiyoda-ku, Tokyo 101-0047
Telephone: (+81)3-6695-2450 Fax: (+81)3-6695-2579
sales@schottjapan.com http://www.schottjapan.com

（価格には消費税が含まれておりません）